Contents

KV-371-050

Introducing Australia

Australia is the largest island in the world. It has an area of 7,682,300 square kilometres. That is about the same size as the whole of Europe. The British Isles would fit into Australia 26 times! In spite of its vast size, only about 17 million people live in Australia.

Australia is also the world's smallest continent. It belongs to a geographic area called Oceania. This area includes Australia's near neighbours New Guinea and New Zealand, and many of the small island nations in the Pacific Ocean. Australia is bordered by the Pacific Ocean in the east, the Indian Ocean in the west and the Southern Ocean in the south.

An old country

Australia is thought to be one of the oldest continents. There was a land bridge to New Guinea until about 50,000 years ago but, as the sea rose, this was flooded and Australia was completely cut off. This is one of the reasons why so many animals and plants can only be found in Australia.

The first inhabitants of Australia were the Aborigines. 'Aboriginal' means 'original inhabitant'. The Maoris in New Zealand and the American Indians in North America are also the Aboriginals (original inhabitants) of their own lands. The Australian Aborigines have kept the name.

Nobody is sure when the Aborigines first arrived in Australia. Archaeologists think that they arrived between 30,000 and 60,000 years ago. It is thought that they either sailed across from South East Asia, or crossed on the land bridge from New Guinea. The Aborigines lived in harmony with the land for many centuries.

Down under

Australia is in the Southern Hemisphere and is sometimes called the land 'down under'. The seasons in the Southern Hemisphere are the reverse of those in Europe and America. Can you imagine celebrating Christmas on a hot, sunny day? The climate differs throughout Australia, but the tropical north only has two seasons, the 'wet' from November to April and the 'dry' from May to October.

Australia is the flattest and the driest continent.

FOCUS ON
AUSTRALIA

Heather Foote

Evans Brothers Limited

Published by Evans Brothers Limited
2A Portman Mansions
Chiltern Street
London W1M 1LE

Design by TJ Graphics
Editor Liz Harman
Map artist Jillian Luff, Bitmap Graphics

Printed in Hong Kong by Dah Hua Printing Co Ltd

ISBN 0 237 51478 8

Acknowledgements
The author and publishers would like to thank the following for
permission to reproduce the photographs:
Australia House: contents, 20 (left), 29 (bottom); Australian
Tourist Commission: title page, 6, 10, 13 (right), 15 (right), 16
(left), 21 (left), 23 (bottom), 25 (top), 28 (right); Bruce Coleman
Limited: 7 (both), 17 (left), 19 (all pictures), 21 (right), 22 (both),
23 (top), 27 (top), 28 (left); Chris Fairclough Colour Library: 15
(left), 17 (right), 25 (bottom left); Robert Harding Picture Library:
12 (left), 16 (right), 18 (right), 25 (right), 27 (bottom), 31 (right);
Hutchison Library: 13 (left), 20 (right), 31 (left); The Image Bank:
4; JS Library: 9 (left), 14 (right); Life File: 9 (right), 12 (right), 14
(left), 18 (left), 25, 26; National Maritime Museum: 8 (top);
National Maritime Museum/Robert Harding Picture Library: 8
(bottom); Promotion Australia, London/Australia House: 11; Dave
Saunders: 30; ZEFA: 29 (top).

Cover Uluru

Title page Aborigines playing the didgeridoo

Opposite The Great Barrier Reef

N

PAPUA
NEW
GUINEA

CORAL
SEA

INDONESIA

TIMOR
SEA

Darwin

*Arnhem
Land*

*Gulf
of
Carpentaria*

Cooktown

Port Douglas
Cairns

Great Barrier Reef

INDIAN
OCEAN

Broome

*Bungle
Bungles*

NORTHERN
TERRITORY

Mount Isa

Townsville

QUEENSLAND

*Great Sandy
Desert*

Great Dividing Range

Tropic of Capricorn

Macdonnell Ranges

Alice Springs

Mt Olga ▲ ▲ *Uluru*

*Simpson
Desert*

WESTERN
AUSTRALIA

A U S T R A L I A

Sunshine Coast
Glasshouse Mts

*Great Victoria
Desert*

Coober Pedy

L. Eyre

Brisbane ■
Gold Coast

SOUTH AUSTRALIA

Darling River

NEW
SOUTH
WALES

Nullarbor Plain

Perth ■

Great Australian Bight

Adelaide ■

Murray River

*Little
Desert*

Great Dividing Range

□ Canberra
▲ *Mt Kosciusko*
*Snowy
Mts*

Sydney ■
Botany Bay

VICTORIA

Melbourne ■

Twelve Apostles

Bass Strait

TASMAN
SEA

INSET MAP (top left):
CHINA
INDIA
PHILIPPINES
PACIFIC
OCEAN
Equator
I N D O N E S I A
PAPUA
NEW
GUINEA
INDIAN
OCEAN
AUSTRALIA
NEW
ZEALAND
SOUTHERN OCEAN

TASMANIA

Hobart ■

—— National border	●	Other towns
—— State border		Mountains
□ Capital city		
■ Major city		Highlands

0   250   500 km
0   125   250 miles

First inhabitants

The Aborigines were mainly nomadic, moving from place to place within their tribal lands, looking for food and trading with other tribes. They hunted animals, such as emu and kangaroo, using spears and boomerangs, killing only what they could eat. The Aborigines brought fire to Australia and regularly burnt the bush to flush out small animals and clear the undergrowth. This controlled burning prevented bushfires. There is evidence that some groups of Aborigines settled permanently to farm the land. Aborigines have always lived in tribal groups. Each group has its own territory, traditions, beliefs and language. Territorial land has always been very important as it is the source of food.

When the Europeans landed in 1788 there were about 300,000 Aborigines in Australia. The Aborigine population fell by 20 per cent after the colonisation of Australia because of European diseases and fighting between the Europeans and the Aborigines. Today, the Aborigine population is 257,333, about one and a half per cent of the total population.

This is an Aboriginal ceremony called a corroboree. People who take part wear special clothes and body paint. The ceremony involves special music. A corroboree might be held to talk to the spirit ancestors, to celebrate or to mourn.

Culture and tradition

There are many Aboriginal religious ceremonies. Some of these ceremonies centred around the tribal totems, which protected the tribe, and others around the spirits of their ancestors. Tribal Aborigines continue these traditional ceremonies today on their tribal land.

Aborigines have a strong oral tradition, mainly relating to the stories from the 'Dreamtime'. The Dreamtime is the past when the Sun and Moon, the land, animals and people were formed. Stories varied from tribe to tribe and were passed on from generation to generation. The stories were depicted in Aboriginal art and re-enacted in tribal ceremonies.

Many Aboriginal words are used in modern Australian English, for example 'billabong' (a pool left behind when a river changes course) and 'boomerang' (a curved stick used for hunting). Many place names are also of Aboriginal origin. Mareeba in Queensland means 'meeting of the waters', and Murrumbidgee River means 'big water'.

Aborigines today

In 1977 the Northern Territory Government gave some land, including Ayers Rock, back to the Aborigine Pitjanjara tribe. Ayers Rock was given its Aboriginal name of Uluru and the area was made into a National Park. There have been many claims for the return of tribal land. The 1992 Marbo Decision recognised that Aborigine tribes had their own land and that the continent had not been 'empty' when European settlers arrived in 1788.

Many more Aborigines now identify with their tribal customs and traditions. All Australians are learning to appreciate the traditions of these original Australians.

Rock paintings and engravings are found at Aboriginal sites throughout Australia.

Many tourists come to see Aboriginal rock paintings.

European Settlement

It is believed that the first visitors to Australia were Chinese and Arabian sailors and traders. Parts of the northern coast are thought to be shown on Chinese maps which are over 2500 years old.

European visitors

Europe had known about 'The Great South Land' since AD 150, when the Greek geographer Ptolemy wondered if there was a *Terra Australis Incognita* (unknown land of the South).

In 1606 a Portuguese navigator, Willem Jansz, landed on the Cape York peninsula and thought it was part of New Guinea. Dutch explorers visited the coast of Australia during the early part of the 17th century but the next organised expedition was not until 1770, when Captain James Cook's expedition sighted the east coast of Australia. Cook then sailed north, charting the coast and landing in Botany Bay before continuing his voyage north. He named many coastal features, including Port Jackson. He next landed at what is now Cooktown, on the river which he named Endeavour, after his ship. He raised the Union Jack on Possession Island and claimed for England the land which he called New South Wales.

The English explorer Captain James Cook

A model of Captain Cook's ship *The Endeavour*

Settlement

Before the American War of Independence, England had regularly sent convicts to the USA. When America refused to accept more convicts, the British Government sent them to Australia. The First Fleet, under the leadership of Captain Arthur Phillip, set out on the long voyage in May 1787, with 11 ships and 778 convicts. The fleet arrived in Botany Bay eight months later but the area was unsuitable for a settlement because it had no fresh water. Captain Phillip sailed on into Port Jackson and found the largest natural harbour in the world. He founded the settlement at Sydney Cove on 26th January 1788.

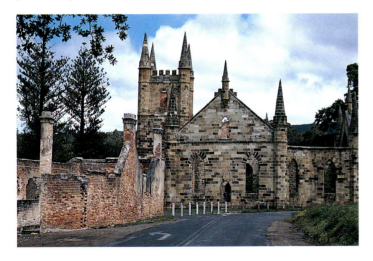

The remains of a church at Port Arthur penal colony, Tasmania. This colony took the most dangerous convicts.

Many fleets of convicts and settlers followed; the colony grew rapidly and a town was built around Sydney Cove. Settlers farmed the land as far west as the Blue Mountains, but they could not cross them. In 1813 the explorers Blaxland, Lawson and Wentworth found a route across to the fertile plains beyond. The settlers took the land they wanted and displaced and killed the Aboriginal people who had lived there. The Aborigines resisted invasion but were no match for the firepower of the settlers.

Other settlements were made at Hobart in 1803, Morton Bay (Brisbane) in 1824, Swan River (Perth) in 1829 and Adelaide in 1836. Convicts did much of the hard work, clearing the land, building roads and houses and working on the farms.

In 1803 Matthew Flinders sailed all the way around the continent and mapped the coastline. He had circumnavigated and mapped the island of Tasmania the year before. After the crossing of the Blue Mountains in 1813, exploration of the vast interior began and many expeditions were carried out. By 1861, explorers had discovered and mapped the basic structure of the Australia we know today.

The transportation of convicts from Britain to Australia was stopped in 1868.

This memorial to Captain Cook stands beside the Endeavour River.

One nation

Separate colonies

For the first 47 years after European settlement, all settlements were ruled by the Governor of New South Wales. Gradually, each one was recognised by England as a separate colony and given limited self-government. All governors were appointed from England and all laws had to be approved by the English Parliament. In 1854 a rebellion against the government at the Eureka Stockade in the Victorian goldfields was put down. But people felt more Australian than English, and began to push for self-rule.

Gold!

In 1851 gold was discovered at Bathurst, New South Wales and then at Ballarat and Bendigo in Victoria. People rushed to the gold fields from all over the country. Many people also came from the USA and China. It is thought that more than 50,000 Chinese immigrated to Australia during the gold rushes.

During the gold rush, gold thieves held up banks and coaches carrying gold. They were called bushrangers and the most famous bushranger was Ned Kelly. Ned Kelly's career ended in a shoot-out with police in which he wore a suit of armour. He was captured, tried and hung in Melbourne in 1880, but he became an Australian legend.

Re-enacting 'panning' for gold at Sovereign Hill Historic Park

Federation

By the late 1880s most people wanted a united Australia rather than separate colonies. Henry Parkes convinced Australians that they should come together as one nation. On 1st January 1901 the Federation of Australia, a federation of six states, came into being. In 1911 New South Wales gave some land to the Federal Government to become the capital of the country. It was called Canberra after an Aboriginal word which means 'meeting place' (see page 12).

At war

When Europe went to war in 1914, Australians and New Zealanders (ANZACs) joined the British side. They fought in many places, but are particularly remembered for the battle at Gallipoli in which almost 8000 Australians died. ANZAC Day (April 25th) is a national holiday.

Australia again sent troops to Europe when war broke out in 1939. This left Australia undefended when the Japanese entered the war and began to move south. Darwin was bombed in 1942, and Australians fought with American troops through the Pacific region.

Since the Second World War, Australian troops have fought in Malaya with the British, and in Korea and Vietnam with the Americans.

ANZAC day parade

Immigration

The first wave of immigrants to Australia were the convicts and settlers from all parts of the British Isles. They were followed by Chinese immigrants during the gold rushes. Then a small group of Germans immigrated to Australia in the early 19th century, seeking religious freedom. They settled in the Barossa Valley in South Australia and began Australia's wine industry.

After Darwin was bombed in the Second World War, the Government decided that the population should be increased so that Australia could be defended from invasion. The Government offered financial assistance to people who wanted to move to Australia. In the 20 years after the war about two and a half million immigrants arrived. About 50 per cent of these people were from Britain, but there were large numbers from southern Europe, Italy and Greece. Melbourne is said to be the third largest Greek city in the world! Since the 1970s the largest numbers of immigrants have come from Asia, Vietnam, Thailand and Cambodia.

Over the years, immigrants have brought their customs and traditions to Australia with them. This has created a multicultural society. It has encouraged European Australians to appreciate other cultures, including the Aboriginal culture.

Towns and cities

Australia is the most urbanised country in the world and about 85 per cent of the population live in cities or towns. Most of these are close to the coast, except for the capital, Canberra. Larger cities and towns usually have a central business district surrounded by sprawling suburbs. The small number of people who do not live in urban areas are scattered around Australia, farming, mining and working in the tourist trade. About half of the Aborigines now live in towns and cities, the remainder living on tribal land. The majority of Australians own their own home, which usually consists of a single-storey property with its own plot of land.

The National Capital

Canberra is in the Australian Capital Territory (ACT). Its name originally comes from an Aboriginal word 'kamberra' meaning 'meeting place'. The city of Canberra was planned by an American architect, Walter Burley Griffin, in 1911. He planned this new city around Lake Burley Griffin, half way between Sydney and Melbourne. Canberra is one of three specially-designed capitals in the world and is the political and administrative centre of Australia. The first Parliament met in Canberra in 1927.

State Capitals

Sydney, Melbourne, Adelaide, Perth, Brisbane, Hobart and Darwin are all

Australia's Parliament Building in Canberra, seen accross Lake Burley Griffin

Hobart, Tasmania, with Mount Wellington in the background

capital cities. They are all situated on or very near the coast, each with nearby port facilities. These are the administrative, political and cultural centres of their state or territory. Their histories are based on the European settlements which took place not much more than 200 years ago. In world-wide terms, they are all relatively new cities.

Sydney

Sydney is the oldest and largest city with a population of about four million and covers the same area as Greater London. It is the commercial centre of Australia. With its cosmopolitan atmosphere, intricate coastline and nearby national parks, Sydney provides many opportunities for the relaxed, outdoor lifestyle typical of most Australians.

Melbourne is Australia's second largest city and, among other things, is famous for the Melbourne Cup horse race and is the home of 'Aussie Rules' football. Perth, in Western Australia, is one of the most isolated cities in the world. The nearest city is Adelaide, 2700 kilometres away.

Darwin was originally known as Palmerstown until 1913, when it was renamed after Charles Darwin the naturalist. A severe cyclone destroyed the city in 1974 but it has now been rebuilt into a modern city with stronger buildings.

Towns
Most towns in Australia owe their origins to the primary industries of mining, farming and fishing. Mount Isa, Coober Pedy, Ballarat and Broken Hill are all towns founded on mineral deposits. Some, like Weipa and Newman, have been specifically built and paid for by the mining companies for the people who work there.

A 'dry boat' race in the dry river bed at Henley on Todd Regatta, Alice Springs

Alice Springs, in central Australia, originally provided fresh water in an otherwise arid area and was used as a supply station for the overhead telegraph line between South Australia and Europe. It is now a popular tourist centre.

Towns along the Gold and Sunshine Coasts have always attracted tourists. Towns in the southern Australian Alps serve as ski-resorts during the winter months. Other towns like Cairns, Port Douglas and Townsville have become increasingly reliant on the tourist trade and provide a wide range of services for visitors.

A land of contrasts

Although Australia is the smallest continent in the world, it is the sixth largest country. Approximately two thirds of Australia is desert. Australians call the desert the 'outback'. The wooded areas close to the coast, and the thinly wooded plains beyond are called the 'bush'.

The coast

The coastline of Australia is 36,735 kilometres long and much of it takes the form of small sandy bays. There are also long stretches of beach and the two longest beaches are Ninety Mile Beach in Victoria and Eighty Mile Beach in Western Australia.

Some areas of the coast have become large holiday resorts. One of the most popular is the Gold Coast, a 32 kilometre stretch of beach in southern Queensland.

The coast has many river estuaries and mangroves, particularly in the north. These are home to a wide range of animals, including the salt-water crocodile.

Islands

There are many islands off the coast of Australia. Tasmania is the largest and was originally joined to the mainland, as were some of the reef islands, like Hinchenbrook Island and Magnetic Island. Islands, like Kangaroo Island and the large islands in the Great Barrier Reef have communities living on them.

Deserts and lakes

Australia's deserts include the Little Desert in Victoria and the Great Sandy Desert in Western Australia. These deserts contain some very unusual rock formations, like Uluru, the Olgas and the Bungle Bungles.

Surfer's Paradise is a famous Gold Coast beach.

Pinnacles of rock in a desert area

The Bungle Bungles are in an area rich in minerals.

In the middle of the deserts is a central basin which is below sea level and is thought to have been an inland sea. Lake Eyre, the biggest lake in Australia, is found here. When full, Lake Eyre covers an area of about 9300 square kilometres.

Mountains and rivers

The main Australian mountain range is the Great Dividing Range, which runs down the east coast from Cape York to Victoria. At 2230 metres, Mount Kosciusko is the highest peak in Australia but it is only about a quarter the height of Mount Everest. Some ranges in Western Australia are thought to be formed from some of the oldest rocks known and are rich in mineral deposits.

Because of the lack of rainfall, many of the rivers which rise (start) in the north are sometimes dry. The Murray River is the longest river in Australia. It rises in a section of the Great Dividing Range called the Snowy Mountains and enters the sea 2590 kilometres later, near Adelaide.

Rainforests

Despite being such a dry continent, Australia has many rainforests along the Great Dividing Range. These are caused by rainclouds hitting the range. The tropical rainforest in north Queensland is home to many unique plants and animals, including some spectacular ferns, unusual birds like the Cassowary, and beautiful butterflies. Many people are working hard to preserve these rainforests and protect the animals and plants.

Walking is popular in the rainforests, where many unusual plants and animals can be seen.

Natural wonders

There are many unusual and ancient rock formations throughout the interior of Australia. There are also a number of other natural wonders which have become famous around the world and attract large numbers of tourists every year.

Great Barrier Reef

This is one of the Seven Wonders of the World and is the world's largest coral reef.

The Great Barrier reef

It took millions of years to grow and is still living today. The reef extends for 2000 kilometres down the coast of Queensland and has grown up 250 metres from the ocean floor in places. Over 2000 species of fish, 300 species of coral and over 50 different birds live on or around the reef, which is the largest but most fragile ecosystem on Earth. The reef is threatened by human activities like oil exploration, sand mining and big game fishing. The huge number of tourists also causes damage and pollution but, because tourism brings so much wealth, there is a strong desire to protect the reef from further damage. The Great Barrier Reef Marine Park Authority was established to protect the reef. They advise tourists not to break off pieces of coral or collect shells as souvenirs. The reef is also attacked by a natural enemy, the crown of thorns starfish, which eats the coral and can damage large areas.

The spectacular and varied marine life on the reef attracts thousands of tourists every year.

The Devil's Marbles

Glowing red when the Sun sets, these massive boulders have been eroded into huge balls by the wind and rain. Many Aborigines believe they were left by a Dreamtime creature called the Rainbow Serpent.

Wave Rock

A granite rock in Western Australia which looks like a huge wave that has turned to stone. It has been made smooth by the wind and has coloured bands formed by the rain washing chemicals from the soil down the rock (leaching).

Wave Rock showing the effects of leaching by rain

Uluru

This huge single rock sticking up out of the flat desert area of central Australia was formerly known as Ayers Rock. It is nine kilometres around the base and geologists believe it is around 600 million years old. This is a sacred place to the Pitjanjara tribe. They believe that it was formed by two boys playing in the mud after a severe rain storm. In 1977 this area was recognised as Aboriginal land and so became known as Uluru again. It is one of the best-known tourist attractions in Australia and can be seen on the cover of this book.

Glasshouse Mountains

In south east Queensland these mountains rise almost vertically from the flat plains. They are the cores of extinct volcanoes. They were called Glasshouse mountains by James Cook because when he first saw them from the sea he noticed reflections from their sheer sides.

Twelve Apostles

Off the southern coast of Victoria there are towers of rock caused by the sea washing away the softer layers of soil and rock around them. Many ships have been wrecked on under-sea rocks.

The Twelve Apostles were formed by erosion caused by the sea and wind.

Animals and plants

Because Australia has many different types of environment and can offer a variety of habitats, it is home to a wide range of different animals and plants.

Marsupials

Marsupials are mammals which have a body pouch in which to suckle and protect their babies until they are old enough to look after themselves. Kangaroos, koalas, possums, wombats, echidnas and the duck-billed platypus are all marsupials.

A grey kangaroo with her baby, a joey, in her pouch

The red kangaroo is the largest marsupial. It can hop along at almost 50 kilometres per hour with the aid of powerful back legs and its strong, thick tail provides balance. Kangaroos and their smaller cousins, wallabies, are most active at dusk and dawn and spend most of the day resting in the shade.

Koalas are marsupials and not bears as some people think. They are shy creatures, eating only eucalyptus leaves and living and sleeping in the branches of eucalyptus trees. The name koala comes from an Aboriginal word meaning 'no drink' because they very rarely drink, obtaining most of their water from eucalyptus leaves.

The echidna and the platypus are unusual because they are mammals which lay eggs. The platypus is probably the strangest living creature, with its large flat

A duck-billed platypus swimming underwater

tail, webbed feet, duck's bill and furry body. It burrows in the banks of rivers and hunts underwater for worms, shrimps and molluscs. It keeps these in pouches in its cheeks until it can reach the surface and swallow them.

Reptiles

Having tropical or sub-tropical temperatures, Australia is home to over 200 species of snake, some of which are the most deadly in the world. The fierce snake and the taipan, found in northern areas, are the most dangerous.

The salt-water crocodile of northern Australia can be as long as seven and a half metres. It is aggressive and has been known to attack people.

The bearded dragon, another fierce-looking reptile, is actually harmless to humans. This one is seen eating a grasshopper.

Birds
Australia boasts a huge variety of colourful birdlife. The emu, the second largest living bird, cannot fly and is almost two metres tall. Kookaburras are the largest of the kingfisher family, although they actually eat mice, small reptiles and insects. Their unique 'laughing' call has given this bird the nickname 'laughing jackass'. Brightly coloured parrots, budgerigars, galahs and other tropical birds can also be seen.

The cassowary is a flightless bird, like the emu.

Spiders
Australia has some of the world's most deadly spiders. The funnel-web and the red-back are the best known.

Plant life
There is a variety of plant life to be found, particularly in the tropical regions.

Eucalyptus trees (better known as gum trees) have blue-green leaves which they lose in stages throughout the year. There are a number of different gum trees such as the 'ghost' gum, and the 'coral' gum which has particularly beautiful flowers in the summer. Eucalyptus oil is made from the leaves and can be used in some medicines. The wood of the eucalyptus is also used for timber (see page 23).

The baobab tree is also called the bottle tree. It stores water in its trunk and can survive in hot, dry conditions.

Natural resources

Australia produces its own supplies of energy from water, coal, gas and the Sun.

Australia is the largest exporter of coal and alumina in the world. Alumina is made from bauxite and is used to make aluminium. Australia is also the second largest exporter of iron-ore. There are huge deposits of other minerals such as copper, lead, silver, gold, zinc, manganese, diamonds and uranium. Together, they make up a quarter of all Australian exports.

The underground copper mines at Mount Isa

Mining sites are usually in harsh, isolated areas, far away from the nearest town or city but many towns have been specially built by the mining companies to provide homes for miners (see page 13).

In the past, mining companies have often been in conflict with the Aborigines because much of the mineral wealth is found in parts of the country which the Aborigines believe to be sacred. In recent years, the Aborigines have been involved in discussions about prospecting and the income from mining.

Iron-ore

Mount Whaleback is one of the largest iron-ore mining sites in Western Australia and the landscape is bright red due to the rich deposits of iron. The miners of Mount Whaleback live in Newman, a purpose-built town about 5 kilometres away.

The Mount Newman open-cast iron-ore mine

Gold

Although gold is no longer the only important mineral, Australia is the fourth largest exporter of gold in the world. Unlike the gold diggers of the past, who panned for gold, miners now use machines to extract this heavy metal from the ground. In some places, the 'tailings' – the waste left over after gold is mined – are being re-excavated. This is because modern technology now allows smaller pieces of gold to be extracted.

Precious stones

Opals are translucent gemstones found in a variety of colours and used for making jewellery. The town of Coober Pedy grew where opals were mined. It is unusual because many people live in underground homes called 'dugouts'. This is more comfortable because the temperatures are so high during the day and cold at night. Coober Pedy is an Aboriginal name, meaning 'place where white man lives underground'. When tourists visit Coober Pedy, they stay in an underground hotel.

The Cave Hotel, Coober Pedy

Diamonds have only been mined in the Kimberley region of Western Australia for the last 20 years. They are mostly low-grade diamonds used in industry. In the far north west, the Australians are hoping that Smoke Creek will become the world's largest diamond field.

Water

Australia is the driest separate land mass on Earth. In such a dry, hot country, water is a very important resource. Enormous amounts of rain and snow fall at certain times of the year but there are also long periods of drought. There is a need to control the use of water and save it for those dry periods. The Snowy River and Murray-Darling Basin Projects are just two of the important systems developed to save water using dams, locks, weirs and power stations.

Solar Energy

The Sun is a relatively cheap and environmentally friendly source of energy. Australians are increasingly using solar heating to supplement other forms of power. Most new houses and factories are built with solar panels in the roof.

Many Australian houses have solar panels set in the roof.

Farming and industry

Farming has declined slightly in importance because of the increase in mining and manufacturing. However it still produces one third of the country's income from exports. The most important agricultural products are wool, beef and wheat but sugar, wine, fish, rice, tobacco and a wide range of fruits are also important to the economy.

Merino sheep being sheared

Sheep and cattle

There are ten times more sheep than people in Australia! Australia is the world's largest exporter of sheep. Very few people work on the farms however, even though each 'sheep station' covers a huge area. Wild dogs, called dingoes, are kept away from the sheep by long stretches of fence which have to be repaired regularly. As cold air comes in from the Antarctic, farmers in the southeast of Australia have

to be ready for sudden drops in temperature which can kill new-born lambs.

Cattle can survive in hotter areas than sheep, but they also require vast areas of land. Cattle from India have been cross-bred with European species to produce animals which survive the harsh climate. In order to 'muster' or herd the animals, farmers use helicopters, motorbikes, horses and two-way radios.

Crops

Wheat and barley are grown throughout the year. Farmers take out insurance policies against hail which can badly damage their crops. Sugar cane, mangoes, bananas, ginger, paw paws and pineapples are grown in the wet tropical areas of

The pineapple harvest in Queensland

Queensland. Further south, in drier conditions, citrus fruits grow well, with apples, pears, peas and potatoes thriving in more temperate regions.

Vineyards in the Hunter Valley

Grapes are grown throughout Australia and wine is exported all over the world. Certain areas of Australia have proved to have excellent conditions for growing grapes and wine-making has become an important industry in recent years.

Forestry and fishing

There are some commercial forests of softwood trees such as pine, which produce timber for furniture, floorboards and paper manufacture. The tree most often used is the eucalyptus which produces hardwood for use in building and industry. A wide variety of seafood, including tuna, salmon, prawns and lobsters, is caught in Australia's rich coastal waters where the fishing industry is growing in importance.

Manufacturing industry

Australia has a broad range of industries and is self-sufficient in most consumer goods. The plentiful supply of minerals has led to industrial plants at the ports in all States. There are also car-assembly plants, computer and plastics manufacturers, ship-building and engineering works.

The abundance of seafood, fruit, meat and dairy products has led to the development of the canning and food-processing industry. Much of this production goes for export.

Tourism

Over recent years, tourism has become Australia's single biggest industry. Foreigners and Australians enjoy exploring Australia, which can offer rivers, mountains, rainforests, deserts and beaches. Tourism brings much wealth and employment to Australia, particularly to its many coastal resorts.

Yellow water in Kakadu is a popular and beautiful tourist site.

Transport and communication

Moving goods and people around Australia has always been difficult because of its great size - the distance from Sydney to Perth is the same as the distance from London to Moscow!

Rivers and railways

In the 18th century the Murray and Darling rivers supported a thriving transport industry. Paddle steamers took wool and other farm produce to the port at Victor Harbour, and returned with household goods and farm machinery. Many towns such as Echuca grew up on the river banks. However, river travel was slow and rivers were often dry due to a lack of rain. Gradually, paddle steamers were replaced by railways.

The first steam train ran from Melbourne to Sandridge in 1854. In the late 1800s railways spread rapidly from the main cities. Unfortunately, as each state built its railway separately, the gauge (the distance between the tracks) differed from state to state. This was inconvenient and costly because passengers and goods travelling between states had to be moved from one train to another. It was not until the 1960s that the gauge became standard throughout Australia. Today the railways are used mainly to transport minerals and produce such as grain.

The modern electric railway in Perth

Highways and skyways

Now, most goods are transported throughout the country by road, on semi-trailers or 'roadtrains'. Roadtrains are huge trucks up to four trailers long. There are a number of highways linking the major cities and Highway 1 rings the country and links all of the state capitals.

Most Australians have cars and use them as their main means of travel. In the cities, suburban railways are a common form of transport. Sydney has a monorail, and Melbourne still has a tram network.

Melbourne is the only Australian city with a tram system.

The Australian airline, Qantas was started in Longreach, Queensland in 1923 and is now an international airline. There are two major internal airlines and a number of smaller carriers. Most people travel between the major cities by air. Many cattle stations have their own airstrips for light aircraft.

The flying doctor service has provided airborne medical assistance for people living in the outback since 1928.

Sending messages

Australia was linked to the international telegraph in 1872. Before this, all messages to other countries had to be sent by ship. Communication by radio became available in the 1920s and was particularly useful for those living in the bush. In the early days farmers had two-way radios powered by pedal generators. Now, people in the outback have the same forms of communication as everyone else. Many of these outback links are now powered by solar energy.

Most children in the outback cannot attend school because they live far from the nearest town. They listen to lessons from the school of the air on their radios. Once a year, they meet up with their teachers and fellow pupils.

Daily life

Australia is considered to be part of the 'Western World' and many aspects of daily life are very similar to those in Great Britain or the USA. However, there are many differences, including the hot, sunny climate and Australia's unique landscape and culture.

Language

The official language is English, but Australian English is usually friendly, informal and spoken with a characteristic accent. Nick-names and slang are common, for example, 'pom' or 'pommie' for a British person, 'strides' for men's trousers, 'tucker' for food. Australians shorten many words, such as 'postie' for postman, 'barbie' for barbecue and 'Brissie' for Brisbane.

Religions, holidays and festivals

There are Christians, Muslims, Hindus, Sikhs, Jews and Buddhists in Australia. Most public holidays are Christian, notably Easter and Christmas, but Chinese New Year and other religious festivals are also celebrated. The Aboriginal religions involve the worship of their ancestors, the land and the spirits which inhabit it. These celebrations are often restricted to tribe members only.

Australia Day and ANZAC Day are both national holidays. The former

Australia Day fireworks

commemorates the day Captain Arthur Phillip began the European settlement at Sydney Cove. The latter is very important to most Australians because they remember the thousands who died at Galipoli in Turkey in 1915, during World War I. On Melbourne Cup Day the whole nation seems to stop to watch this famous horse race, but it is only a holiday in Melbourne. Every town and city has its own 'Show Day'.

Sport and recreation

The climate is ideal for outdoor activities. Cricket, horse racing, golf, bowls, tennis, skiing, 'Aussie Rules' football , soccer and rugby are all extremely popular. With easy access to the beaches, water sports such as swimming, sailing, surfing, fishing, wind-surfing, water skiing and scuba diving are also enjoyed by many Australians.

Surfing is a popular sport.

The warm weather means that Australians can have barbecues and picnics outdoors most of the year.

In 1994, bushfires caused damage and loss of wildlife around Sydney.

Living with nature

The hot climate can cause problems. Droughts, bushfires, cyclones and dust-storms are all potentially dangerous, even to those living in the cities. The nature of the rainfall is such that long periods of drought can be followed by severe flooding. Cyclones (tropical storms) develop off the northern and north eastern coasts. People living in these regions receive warnings so that they can prepare emergency supplies, secure vehicles and stay indoors. In 1974 Darwin was destroyed by Cyclone Tracy.

Protection from the Sun

Australians spend a lot of time outdoors in the sunshine. This means they need to protect their skin from the Sun's rays. Australia has the highest level of skin cancer in the world. This is because many Australians are from European races, whose pale skin is not suited to the weather conditions. At school children must wear a hat when playing in the playground. On the beach, people protect their noses and lips with coloured sun block cream. They also wear hats, sunglasses and sunscreen.

Art and literature

Aboriginal art

Aborigines painted using colours which they made from the soil. There are caves throughout Australia which contain many paintings. This ancient people also carved pictures on stone and in wood. Traditional Aboriginal songs, poems and myths are now being recognised and appreciated around the world. Aboriginal musical instruments like the didgeridoo and drums made of hollowed-out tree trunks are used in traditional and modern music. Many writers and artists are inspired by the Aboriginal culture.

The Heidelburg School started outside Melbourne in the 1880s and is famous for training artists who produce beautiful landscape paintings. Before this, Europeans had difficulty representing the unfamiliar landscape. Sidney Nolan is particularly famous for his paintings of Ned Kelly the bushranger. A number of Aborigine painters were successful in following the European style. The best known of them was Albert Namatjira, whose watercolour landscapes are admired throughout the country.

Aborigines playing the didgeridoo, a traditional wooden instrument

European influences

When Europeans settled in Australia, they brought with them different ways of expressing their cultural traditions.

Adelaide's art festival is a famous biannual event.

28

International success

Henry Lawson and AB 'Banjo' Paterson are just two Australian authors famous for writing about life in the bush. In 1975, the novelist Patrick White won the Nobel Prize for Literature.

Talented Australian musicians like John Williams the guitarist, and the pop-group INXS have gained worldwide recognition.

Australia has a successful film and television industry and exports to many countries. Films like *Crocodile Dundee*, *Picnic at Hanging Rock* and *Strictly Ballroom* and television series such as *Neighbours*, *Home and Away* and *The Flying Doctors* have a worldwide audience.

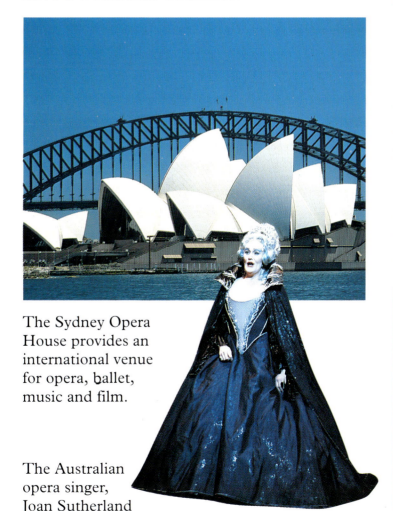

The Sydney Opera House provides an international venue for opera, ballet, music and film.

The Australian opera singer, Joan Sutherland

Many artists and entertainers have gained world renown through the media. They include Mel Gibson, Clive James, Paul Hogan and Barry Humphries as the character Dame Edna Everage.

Children's literature

The famous film *Storm Boy* was based on the children's book written by Colin Thiele. Many other children's books by Australian authors are sold all over the world. The stories are often based on characters associated with the Australian bush. For instance, Snuggle-pot and Cuddle-pie and Bib and Bub are imaginary gum-nut babies (gum nuts grow on eucalyptus treees) and Blinky Bill is a young koala who has many adventures in the bush.

Other stories come from Aboriginal mythology. The Quinkins were the spiritual people of the land. Legends about these were passed down through the generations and are now preserved in book form. They illustrate many aspects of Aboriginal life. The story of The Rainbow Serpent is a story from the Dreamtime and records what some Aborigines believe about the beginning of life.

The National Song

The most famous Australian poem, *Waltzing Matilda* was written by AB 'Banjo' Paterson, while he was staying on a cattle station in New South Wales. This poem is now the National Song and was considered, but rejected, as the National Anthem.

Australia and the world

Like many countries, Australia has been affected by the recession of the 1980s and 90s. Australia is also growing up in a world sense and becoming more involved in world affairs. Australia is a member of organisations such as the Commonwealth, the United Nations, UNESCO and GATT. Australia also has defence links with New Zealand and the USA. Since the Second World War Australia has strengthened links with the USA and fought in the Vietnam War with the US Army. Links with Britain have lessened, particularly as Britain became more involved in the European Community.

Australia's ties have become stronger in the Pacific region and in Asia. In the future Australia will look to Asia for closer friendship and trading links. The trade between Australia and Asian countries has increased dramatically in the last ten years. Japan is Australia's biggest trading partner.

The balance of Australia's trade has altered enormously in the last 20 years. Even in the 1950s Australia was predominantly an agricultural or primary producer, with the country 'riding on the sheep's back'. Wool, wheat and other primary produce are still major exports but the export of minerals has also increased and become very important to Australia's future.

Australia has become a major tourist destination. People come from all over the world to see the unique animals and beautiful landscape. Many of these tourists come from neighbouring Asian countries, particularly from Japan. As more tourists visit Australia, many more people are employed in this industry.

Many Japanese people visit Australia on business and for holidays.

Land rights
The 1992 Marbo Decision from the High Court will make a big difference to

Australia. It will give Australia's original inhabitants, the Aborigines, a larger stake in the future and will enable them to continue their customs and traditions. This will enrich the whole community and will help white and immigrant Australians to work with the Aboriginal people.

more Asian immigrants have arrived. These people and the original inhabitants of the country have never had any ties with Britain. Because of the widespread enthusiasum for a Republic the Australian Government is looking at the Constitutional changes that would be necessary. The Australian people will be asked to vote on this issue before the centenary of the Commonwealth of Australia in the year 2001.

The High Court in Canberra

Australia's stock exchange in Sydney

Australian Republic

During the last 20 years there have been increasing calls for Australia to become a republic. This would mean the head of government would not be the Queen of England, but an elected or appointed Australian. Australia would, however remain a member of the Commonwealth.

Most white Australians are now third or fourth generation Australians with no close ties with Britain or the British crown. Also, since World War II, more non-British Europeans have settled in Australia, and

Olympics 2000

Sydney was successful in its bid to host the Olympics Games in the year 2000. This will be an important celebration for all Australia. It will be an opportunity to show the world how Australia has grown and changed, and how Australia is facing the next century with courage and confidence.

Index and summary

Area of Australia:	7,682,300 square kilometres
Population:	17,414,300 (1991)
Capital:	Canberra
Main towns:	Adelaide, Brisbane, Canberra, Darwin, Hobart, Melbourne, Newcastle, Perth, Sydney, Townsville, Woollongong
Main exports:	Coal, iron ore, wheat, wool, meat
Main imports:	Petroleum, office and electrical machinery, textiles
Main crops:	Wheat, fruit, sugar cane
Highest point:	Mount Kosciusko
Longest river:	Murray River
Official language:	English
Currency:	Australian Dollars
National airline:	Qantas